CALIFORNIA

by Tamra B. Orr

GARETH**STEVENS**
PUBLISHING
A Member of the WRC Media Family of Companies

Please visit our web site at: www.garethstevens.com
For a free color catalog describing Gareth Stevens Publishing's
list of high-quality books and multimedia programs, call
1-800-542-2595 (USA) or 1-800-387-3178 (Canada).
Gareth Stevens Publishing's fax: (414) 332-3567.

Library of Congress Cataloging-in-Publication Data

Orr, Tamra.
    California / Tamra B. Orr.
       p. cm. — (Portraits of the states)
    Includes bibliographical references and index.
    ISBN 0-8368-4621-4 (lib. bdg.)
    ISBN 0-8368-4640-0 (softcover)
    1. California—Juvenile literature. I. Title. II. Series.
    F861.3.O77   2005
    979.4—dc22   2005042612

This edition first published in 2006 by
Gareth Stevens Publishing
A Member of the WRC Media Family of Companies
330 West Olive Street, Suite 100
Milwaukee, WI 53212 USA

This edition copyright © 2006 by Gareth Stevens, Inc.

Editorial direction: Mark J. Sachner
Project manager: Jonatha A. Brown
Editor: Betsy Rasmussen
Art direction and design: Tammy West
Picture research: Diane Laska-Swanke
Indexer: Walter Kronenberg
Production: Jessica Morris and Robert Kraus

Picture credits: Cover, pp. 4, 5, 6, 10, 12, 16, 22, 26 © Corel; pp. 9, 21, 28,
29 © PhotoDisc; p. 11 © Herbert/Getty Images; p. 15 © CORBIS; pp. 24, 25
© Gibson Stock Photography; p. 27 © Michael Zagaris/Getty Images

Printed in the United States of America

1 2 3 4 5 6 7 8 9 09 08 07 06 05

CONTENTS

Words that are defined in the Glossary appear
in **bold** the first time they are used in the text.

On the Cover: Miles of beaches draw surfers from all over the world.
They climb on their boards and head for the waves!

Introduction

It is little wonder that California is called "The Golden State." The state is known for its blue skies, bright sunshine, and sandy beaches. But California is also known for **earthquakes**. It has small ones every year and big ones less often that can destroy buildings and hurt people. But California is such a beautiful place that people don't seem to mind that the earth shakes every once in a while.

California is also known as a place to go to find a better way of life. For many years, settlers have headed there. The Chinese who settled there called California "The Golden Mountain."

The elegant Golden Gate Bridge is considered one of the top ten construction achievements of the twentieth century.

The state flag of California.

CALIFORNIA FACTS

- Became the 31st State: September 9, 1850
- Population (2004): 35,893,799
- Capital: Sacramento
- Biggest Cities: Los Angeles, San Diego, San Jose, San Francisco
- Size: 155,959 square miles (403,934 square kilometers)
- Nickname: The Golden State
- State Tree: California redwood
- State Flower: Golden poppy
- State Animal: California grizzly bear
- State Bird: California valley quail

History

Thousands of years ago, Native Americans came to California. Most Natives lived in large family groups. Everyone had a job to do. Some people spent their days looking for food. They picked wild nuts and berries. They fished in streams and rivers. They picked up acorns and ground them into flour.

The Native Americans lived well. They had plenty of food, and the weather was mild. The population grew. By the mid-1500s, more than 130,000 Native people lived in the area we call California.

The First Visitors

The first **explorers** to see this western area came from Spain. They first saw the land in the mid-1500s. Two hundred years later, the Spanish began to settle the area.

A painting of Yosemite Valley shows some of the beauty found throughout California. Many people came to California for its beauty.

Soldiers built forts. Priests came, too. They built churches known as **missions**. They brought Native Americans to the missions to teach them about the Christian religion. The priests established many missions along the coast.

After 1769, the missions grew quite powerful. Small towns were built around them. Priests forced many Natives to become Christians and to work for them. The Natives had to live inside the crowded missions. Many of them became sick and died.

In 1821, Mexico won its **independence** from Spain. At that time, California became a part of Mexico. Through the years, the way of life in this area changed as white settlers built ranches and raised cattle. In 1846, the United States went to war with Mexico and won. In 1850, the United States claimed California as its own.

A Spot of Gold

In January 1848, a man

named James Marshall was digging in a stream. He was making it deeper so his partner, Johann Sutter, could build a sawmill there. Marshall spotted something shining in the water. He had found gold!

It took six months for the news about gold to spread. There was no quick way to tell people because there were no telephones or cars. In December 1848, the president of the United States gave a speech about finding gold in California. People got very excited. They packed their bags and headed to California. They wanted to search for fortune. Others went to open new stores. They knew people would need food, clothing, and other goods. This wave of people moving to California was called the Gold Rush. Because the Gold Rush happened in 1849, the people who went there were called "Forty-Niners."

Famous People of California

Johann Augustus Sutter

Born: February 15, 1803, Kandern, Baden (now Germany)

Died: June 18, 1880, Washington, D.C.

Johann Sutter was a businessman. He came to California in 1839. The Mexican government had given him a lot of land. He built a fort. It was a place for settlers to stop and rest. Sutter hired Native Americans to help him. He hoped to create a city. He wanted to call it Sutterville. After James Marshall found gold, settlers took over Sutter's land. They stole his cattle. They took his tools and supplies. In the end, he died without a home or money.

Thousands of people poured into California, and it began to grow. Some people came to California from China. They were not always treated well. Some Americans did not like Chinese people coming to their country. They did not want them taking jobs. The Chinese knew they were not liked. Many of them moved to San Francisco. There, they set up an area where they felt safer and more at home. It was called **Chinatown**.

Here Comes the Train!

Many Chinese worked to build a railroad track across the country. This building project was called the **Transcontinental** Railroad. Building the railroad was a dangerous job. It involved laying tracks over cliffs that soared into the air. It also meant blasting through rock

IN CALIFORNIA'S HISTORY

Time to Get Organized
In September 1849, forty-eight men from California got together. With all of the new people coming to their area, they needed a system of government. They were tired of waiting for Congress's help to do this, so they met in Monterey and did it themselves. A year later, the president made California the nation's thirty-first state.

After the Gold Rush ended, many towns were left deserted, such as this one in the Sierra Nevadas. The gold so many had hoped for was never found.

9

with explosives. Many workers died before the track was done. If it had not been for the hard work of the Chinese, however, the track would have taken much longer to build.

An amazing thing happened in Utah in May of 1869. The final **spike** for the tracks was hammered in. The Transcontinental Railroad

Trains changed the lives of Californians. They made it possible for people and products to move from one place to another very fast.

was completed. Now trains could travel all the way across the country. Cattle, food, and other products could be sent from one coast to the other. People who lived in the east could finally visit the west more easily. Many people from the east went to California to visit. Some of them stayed.

The population in California kept growing. Native Americans were often

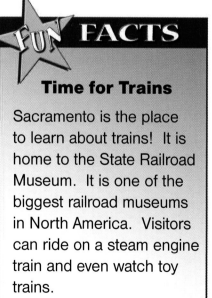

FACTS

Time for Trains

Sacramento is the place to learn about trains! It is home to the State Railroad Museum. It is one of the biggest railroad museums in North America. Visitors can ride on a steam engine train and even watch toy trains.

In hopes of finding a better life, many families came to California. Everything they owned was in their cars.

Crops died, and dirt from the farm fields pushed aside. Many were forced to live far from their homes in specially created areas called **reservations**.

Blowing in the Wind

In the 1930s, some states in the middle of the country were in trouble. It did not rain there for a long time.

blew in the air. The big area where this happened started to be called the Dust Bowl. Families who lived there did not know what to do. They were farmers who could no longer farm. Finally, many headed west. They had heard California was a good place to find jobs.

IN CALIFORNIA'S HISTORY

In 1849, California gave itself a state **motto**. The motto is "Eureka!" This is a Greek word. It means, "I have found it!" It refers to the first people who discovered gold in the state.

Growing Up

Life in California changed during the 1940s. The country was fighting World War II. In World War II, the United States fought Japan and other countries.

In 1989, game three of the San Francisco—Oakland World Series was stopped when the earth began to shake. It is the first time in history that a game was called due to an earthquake.

FUN FACTS

When the Earth Moves

Experts report that there are more than five hundred thousand tremors in California every year. The San Andreas Fault line is found here. It is a large crack in the earth's crust, far under the ground. It is the source of many earthquakes. One of the biggest disasters in the state's history was the San Francisco Earthquake of 1906. At least seven hundred people were killed and thousands were injured.

Japanese Americans were looked at with suspicion during this time. They were taken from their homes and sent to live in camps. The camps were overcrowded. They did not have enough food. Many Japanese lost their homes and property. Two and one-half years after they were opened, the U.S. president closed down all the camps. In 1988, the U.S. Congress apologized for what had been done. They gave money to some Japanese people.

In the 1960s, the United States was in a race to be the first country to land people on the Moon. California began to build parts for rocket ships. Then, in the 1980s, people became interested in computers. California soon became an important place where computers are built.

★ ★ ★ Time Line ★ ★ ★

1530s	Spanish explorers see California for the first time.
1769	California is settled by Spain.
1821	California is ruled by Mexico.
1846	The United States fights a war with Mexico.
1848	Gold is discovered in California.
1848	The United States takes California from Mexico.
1849	People flock to California to find gold in an event known as the "Gold Rush."
1850	California becomes a state.
1869	Trains connect California to the east.
1930s	The Dust Bowl hits parts of the country.
Early 1940s	Japanese Americans are sent to live in camps during World War II.
1989	World Series game between Oakland and San Francisco is stopped because of an earthquake.
1995	Los Angeles earthquake kills fifty-seven people.
2003	Arnold Schwarzenegger is sworn in as governor.
2005	Mud slides kill ten people in La Conchita.

People

No other state in the country has more people than California. People have been drawn to its shores, farmlands, and cities for years. Today, almost thirty-six million people live in California. Almost three-quarters of them live very close to the coast.

The Earliest Californians

The first people to live in California were Native Americans. Today, more than three hundred thousand still live there. The

Hispanics: In the 2000 U.S. Census, 32.4 percent of the people in California called themselves Latino or Hispanic. Most of them or their relatives came from Spanish-speaking backgrounds. They may come from different racial backgrounds.

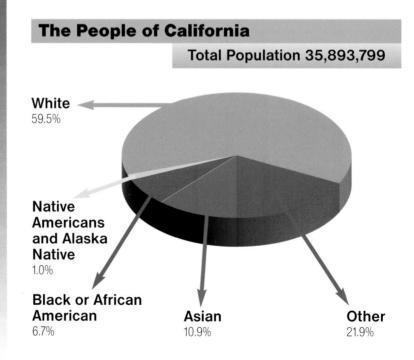

The People of California

Total Population 35,893,799

White
59.5%

Native Americans and Alaska Native
1.0%

Black or African American
6.7%

Asian
10.9%

Other
21.9%

Percentages are based on 2000 Census.

The skyscrapers of Los Angeles soar up so high, they look as if they could touch the clouds.

state has more Native Americans than any other state in the country.

Most of the first Europeans to come to California were from Spain. White people still make up the largest group in the state. When the Gold Rush began, thousands flooded into the state from across the nation and the world. Then trains connecting the east side of the country to the west brought even more people. Ranchers, hunters, and store owners moved there. Farmers came to raise cattle and grow crops.

Many Chinese came, too. They hoped to find jobs and a chance for a better life.

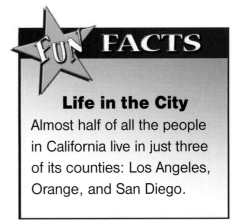

FUN FACTS

Life in the City

Almost half of all the people in California live in just three of its counties: Los Angeles, Orange, and San Diego.

One place you will always find people in California is at the beaches. Everyone comes to soak up some sun and play in the salty ocean water.

Today, more than three million Asian Americans live in California.

Almost one-third of all Californians are Latinos. They came from Mexico and other countries in Latin America. Like others, Latinos come looking for jobs and a good place to raise their families. More people of Mexican **ancestry** live in Los Angeles than in any other city in the world except Mexico City, Mexico.

Californians have not always wanted people from other countries to move to their state, however. A few times, they have passed laws to **limit** or stop different groups from coming there. The groups included Chinese, Japanese, and Latinos. Today, people in California still argue about whether this kind of law is good or bad.

Education

Learning is very important to the people of California.

Famous People of California

Arnold (Alois) Schwarzenegger

Born: July 30, 1947, Thal bei Graz, Austria

In 2003, Arnold Schwarzenegger became California's thirty-eighth governor. He did not have to win an election to become famous, however. Most Americans already knew his name very well. Years before, he had been a great body-builder. Then, he began acting in movies. In 1984, he starred in *The Terminator*. He made other movies, too. When he ran for governor, his fans still recalled the strong man he had played on screen years before. Many still called him "The Terminator."

California has more than one thousand libraries. It has more colleges than any other state. It also has well-known **universities** such as the University of California at Los Angeles (UCLA), Stanford University, the California Institute of Technology, and the University of California at Berkeley.

It is a law in California that children between the ages of six and fifteen have to go to school.

Religion

About three-quarters of the people in California are Christians. Many of these Christians are Catholics. Others are Protestants. More than one million Jews live in the state, too. Smaller numbers are Muslim, Buddhist, or another religion.

The Land

California is known for its warm sunshine and ocean coastline. But snow can also be found in the state on its many mountain tops. Desserts can be found in California, too.

California is on the Pacific Ocean. The coastline is long, rugged, and very beautiful. Many visitors go to the California coast for vacation.

The state also has big mountain ranges. Forests of pine and fir cover some of them. Others are bare. There are even some old volcanoes there! They stopped spewing fire and rock long ago. Now they are quiet.

Waterways and Deserts

California has large rivers and lakes. The Sacramento and the San Joaquin are the longest rivers that are completely in California. They run hundreds of miles through the state. The flat land along these rivers is good for farming. The Colorado River runs along the state's southeastern border. It brings water for farmers and homes.

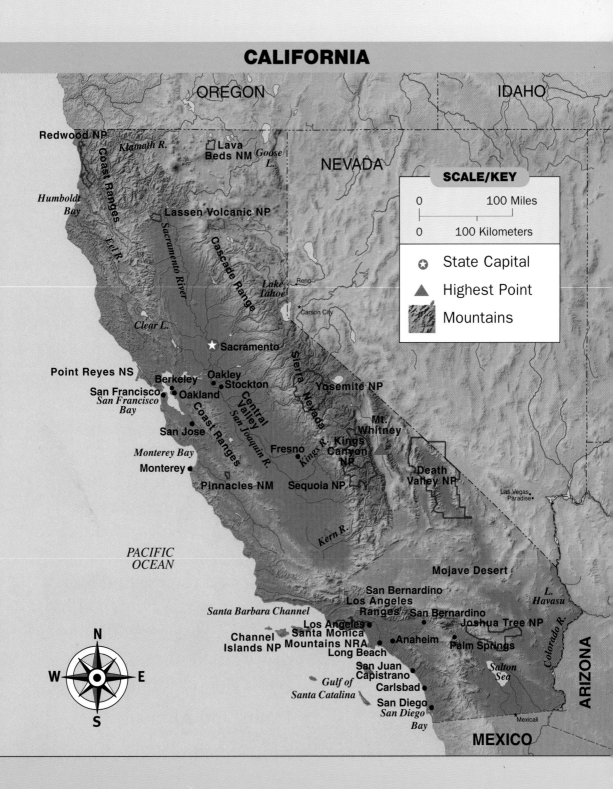

CALIFORNIA

OREGON

IDAHO

NEVADA

Redwood NP

Klamath R.

Lava Beds NM

Goose L.

Coast Ranges

Humboldt Bay

Lassen Volcanic NP

Eel R.

Sacramento River

Cascade Range

Clear L.

Lake Tahoe

Reno

Carson City

★ Sacramento

Sierra Nevada

Point Reyes NS

Berkeley

Oakley

Stockton

Yosemite NP

San Francisco

Oakland

San Francisco Bay

Central Valley

Coast Ranges

San Joaquin R.

San Jose

Fresno

Kings R.

Kings Canyon NP

Mt. Whitney

Monterey Bay

Monterey

Pinnacles NM

Sequoia NP

Death Valley NP

Las Vegas
Paradise

Kern R.

PACIFIC OCEAN

Mojave Desert

L. Havasu

San Bernardino
Los Angeles Ranges

Santa Barbara Channel

San Bernardino

Joshua Tree NP

Los Angeles

Santa Monica Mountains NRA

Anaheim

Palm Springs

Colorado R.

Channel Islands NP

Long Beach

San Juan Capistrano

Salton Sea

ARIZONA

Gulf of Santa Catalina

Carlsbad

San Diego

San Diego Bay

Mexicali

MEXICO

SCALE/KEY

| 0 | 100 Miles |
| 0 | 100 Kilometers |

★ State Capital

▲ Highest Point

Mountains

N
W E
S

19

There are more than eight thousand lakes in California. Lake Tahoe is the deepest one. It is located high in the mountains.

California is also home to several deserts. The Mojave Desert is the biggest. Death Valley is the hottest and driest place in the United States. Death Valley got its name from a group of Forty-Niners who traveled through it on their way to the Gold Rush.

When It Rains

California is a big state. It has many kinds of weather. The low deserts have sunshine almost every day of the year. The deserts are hot in the summer and warm in the winter. They get almost no rain. It's different in the mountains. They get cold in the winter and have plenty of snow.

Major Rivers

Colorado River
1,450 miles (2,333 km) long

Sacramento River
320 miles (515 km) long

San Joaquin River
350 miles (563 km) long

Some say it never rains in California. That is not quite true, especially along the coast. Sometimes the rain falls so fast and hard that it causes mud slides. The ground gets soft and turns into mud. Sometimes the sliding mud blocks roads. Other times, it pushes houses off their foundations. Some homes are crushed by mud. In January 2005, ten people died in mud slides in the city of La Conchita.

Plants and Animals

Almost half of California is covered by forests. Trees

The north coast of California is home to some of the biggest trees in the world. These include the redwoods. They grow hundreds of feet tall. Some are even so large that cars can drive right through the trunks.

called redwoods are the tallest trees in the world. Sequoias are very tall, too. They are among the oldest living trees in the world. Golden poppies are the state flower. They pop up in the valleys.

The state animal is the grizzly bear. No grizzlies have been seen in California for almost one hundred years, however. The state is home to many other animals, too. Foxes, deer, and squirrels live in the forests. Black bears and elk live in the mountains.

Deserts are home to snakes and lizards. Otters and sea lions live on the coast.

Warblers, jays, and wood-peckers are found all over the state. Bigger birds include **condors**. Condors are the largest birds in the country. They fly very fast.

FUN FACTS

That's One Big Tree

California has many huge trees. The biggest is the General Sherman Tree. It is a giant sequoia. It weighs more than 6,000 tons. It stands almost 275 feet (84 m) high.

Economy

Californians have many different types of jobs. Some of these jobs are in tourism. People visit the beaches. They go to Disneyland. They stay in hotels. They eat in restaurants. All of these places need people to work at them.

Going to Work

Almost half of the people with jobs in California help others. Some are teachers. Others wait on tables or cook food. Still others work in hotels or hospitals.

Many fruits and vegetables are grown in California. Strawberries and lettuce are important crops. They are shipped all

When people think of California, they often think of movies. This "Hollywood" sign was put up in 1923. In 1978, it was repaired and still looks over the city of Los Angeles today.

Have You Seen the Artichoke Queen?

The city of Castroville is known as the Artichoke Capital of the World. In 1947, the Artichoke Queen was a young woman named Norma Jean Mortenson. She became Marilyn Monroe, one of the world's most famous actresses.

other state. It is also known for its orange and grapefruit orchards and for its dairy farms.

For the last one hundred years, Hollywood has been known for making movies and television shows. Many people have jobs behind the camera. They paint and build **sets**. They work the cameras. They operate the lights. Together, they create a movie!

over the country. California grows more grapes than any

How Money Is Made in California

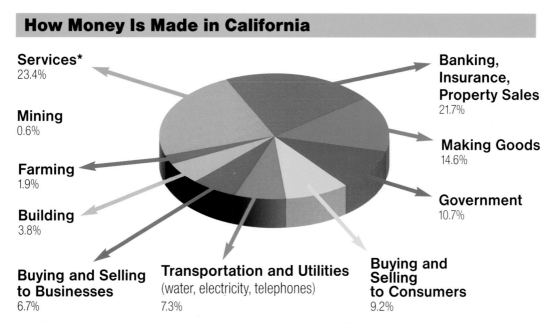

Services*
23.4%

Mining
0.6%

Farming
1.9%

Building
3.8%

Banking, Insurance, Property Sales
21.7%

Making Goods
14.6%

Government
10.7%

Buying and Selling to Businesses
6.7%

Transportation and Utilities
(water, electricity, telephones)
7.3%

Buying and Selling to Consumers
9.2%

* Services include jobs in hotels, restaurants, auto repair, medicine, teaching, and entertainment.

Government

Sacramento is California's capital city. This is where the state's leaders work. The government is divided into three parts. They are the executive, legislative, and judicial branches. Each one is very important.

Executive Branch

The head of the executive branch is the governor. He is helped by the lieutenant governor. Both of them are helped by the **cabinet**. It is the executive branch's job to make sure state laws are carried out.

The California State Capitol is in the city of Sacramento. It is 145 years old!

Legislative Branch

The legislative branch has the job of making state laws. This branch is divided into two parts. One is the Senate, and the other is the Assembly. The two parts work together.

Judicial Branch

The judicial branch is made up of judges and courts. The role of judges is to **interpret** the state's laws. When people are accused of committing crimes, the courts help decide whether they are guilty or innocent.

County Governments

California is divided into fifty-eight counties. Each

Seventeen governors have lived in this fancy house, which used to be the governor's mansion. Today it is a museum.

county has its own form of government. California also has about 470 cities. Under a process called "home rule," the people of these cities are allowed to make some of their own rules.

CALIFORNIA'S STATE GOVERNMENT

Executive		Legislative		Judicial	
Office	Length of Term	Body	Length of Term	Court	Length of Term
Governor	4 years	Senate (40 members)	4 years	Supreme	
Lieutenant Governor	4 years	House of Representatives		(1 chief Justice & 6 judges)	12 years
		(80 members)	2 years	Appeals	12 years

Things to See and Do

There is plenty to do and see in California. It is hard to know where to start. Families like to visit Disneyland and the San Diego Zoo. Surfers and swimmers head for the beaches. Hikers and campers go to Yosemite National Park and other natural places. Shoppers hop on San Francisco's cable cars. Movie fans take tours through Hollywood.

Play Ball!

California is a great place for sports lovers. They can watch the San

Miles of beaches draw surfers from all over the world. They climb on their boards and head for the waves.

26

Walt Disney

Born: December 5, 1901, Chicago, Illinois

Died: December 15, 1966, Los Angeles, California

When he was a boy, Walt Disney loved to draw. He kept on drawing after he grew up. One day, he drew a picture of a mouse. He called him Mickey and put him in a black-and-white cartoon movie called *Steamboat Willie*. This mouse was a hit! Walt kept drawing. He created new characters. With help from his brother Roy, he made movies about his cartoon characters. In 1955, Walt and Roy opened Disneyland. Today, millions of people come to visit this theme park every year.

Francisco 49ers, San Diego Chargers, or Oakland Raiders play football. They can see Los Angeles Lakers, Los Angeles Clippers, Golden State Warriors, or Sacramento Kings shoot baskets. Baseball fans can watch the Los Angeles Angels of Anaheim, Los Angeles Dodgers, Oakland Athletics, San Diego Padres, or San Francisco Giants. They can see a hockey game with the Mighty Ducks of Anaheim, San Jose Sharks, or Los Angeles Kings. College

The famous 49ers have won five Super Bowls so far.

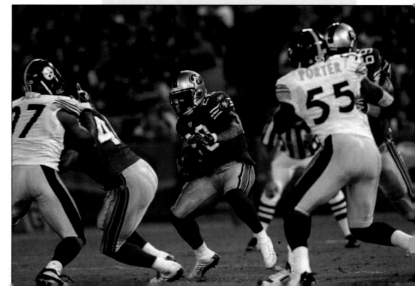

Famous People of California

Maurice "Mac" McDonald

Born: November 26, 1902, Manchester, New Hampshire

Died: December 11, 1971, Palm Springs

Dick McDonald

Born: February 16, 1909, Manchester, New Hampshire

Died: July 14, 1998, Manchester, New Hampshire

These brothers had a dream. They wanted to be millionaires. As young men, they moved to California. World War II ended. They opened a restaurant in San Bernardino. There, they created the idea of "fast food." In 1953, they came up with a way to get people to see their restaurant. They put a bright yellow arch on the top. They named the place McDonald's. Soon, they built more restaurants in other cities. In 1961, they sold most of them. They became millionaires!

The beauty of old California can still be found in places throughout the state.

football fans look forward to watching the Rose Bowl that is played in the state each year.

Some people like to do more than just watch sports. They like to play them! The mountains are a favorite place for snow skiers. The lakes and rivers attract water skiers, boaters, fishers, or divers.

Come to the Festival

California has many fun events to go to. There is an Almond Festival in Oakley. In Stockton, people go to the Asparagus Festival. It lasts three days!

Sacramento is the place to go for the state fair. Chinatown has a parade on Chinese New Year. San Juan Capistrano has a street fair each year. It is held to welcome back the swallows. These birds fill the sky when they return for the summer.

For thousands of years, people have come to California with hopes and dreams. As the state continues to grow and develop, they will keep

coming. Today, millions of tourists still head west. They come to explore and visit. And some still come looking for a new life in the warm sunshine of California.

One of the favorite ways to travel in San Francisco is by cable car. All the ups and downs of the big hills make for a fun ride.

ancestry — the people in a family who came before

cabinet — a team of people who help a political leader make decisions

Chinatown — an area within a city that is mostly made up of Chinese people

condors — vultures that are the largest birds in the United States

earthquakes — shaking of the earth due to layers of rock far underground rubbing past each other

explorers — people who visit a new land to learn about it

independence — freedom from control by others

interpret — explain the meaning of something

limit — to keep at a certain number or amount

missions — in California, places for priests to spread the Christian religion

motto — a brief way to say what a person or group thinks or believes

reservations — land set apart by the government for a certain purpose

sets — rooms or places where movie or TV scenes are filmed

spike — a very large nail

transcontinental — going across a continent

universities — schools to attend for learning after high school

Books

California Gold Rush. Scholastic History Readers (series). Peter Roop (Scholastic Books)

Earthquake! Milly Lee (Farrar, Straus and Giroux)

Gold Fever. Catherine McMorrow (Random House Books for Young Readers)

Mission San Francisco De Solano (The Missions of California). Allison Stark Draper (Powerkids Press)

Striking It Rich: The Story of the California Gold Rush. Ready to Read (series). Stephen Krensky (Aladdin Books)

Two Bear Cubs: A Miwok Legend from California's Yosemite Valley. Robert D. San Souci (Yosemite Association)

Web Sites

CalCritters: The Animals of California
home.earthlink.net/%7Eboytan/calcritters/index.htm

California Department of Real Estate Kids Page
www.dre.ca.gov/kidlinks.htm

Kids page from the California Department of Transportation
www.dot.ca.gov/kids

Native Californians
home.earthlink.net/~boytan/nativecal/index.htm

INDEX